After the War for Independence

Gerry LaFemina

STEPHEN F. AUSTIN STATE UNIVERSITY PRESS

For more information:
Stephen F. Austin State University Press
P.O. Box 13007 SFA Station
Nacogdoches, Texas 75962
sfapress@sfasu.edu
www.sfasu.edu/sfapress

Managing Editor: Kimberly Verhines
Book Design: Emily Williams

Distributed by Texas A&M Consortium
www.tamupress.com

ISBN: 978-1-62288-941-9

Acknowledgments

The author would like to thank the editors of the following journals for publishing earlier versions of many of these poems.

Blue Mountain Review:	"Big Brown Bat" & "Variation on the Third Law of Motion."
The Common:	"Night Driving"
Florida Review:	"Scenic Overlook, I-68 East, Maryland"
Foundlings:	"Almost"
Fugue:	"Solstice"
Gargoyle:	"Club Soda," "Dog," & "The Last Farmer's Market of the Season"
Italian Americana:	"Boa Constrictor"
Juxtaprose:	"Watching the News I'm Reminded of the New York of Childhood"
Lake Effect:	"Sex & Death to the Age 14"
Los Angeles Review:	"The End of Childhood"
Maryland Literary Review:	"Waking Early to Birdsong I Think of Our History of Loss"
Mockingbird:	"Approaching Thanksgiving," "Derecho," "The Asymmtry of Time," "O Holy Night," & "Porcupine"
Mutata Re:	"First Church of the Long-Haul Trucker" & "Let the Evidence for the Divine be Found"
One:	"Kind of Blue"
One Art:	"It's Christmas, the Turkey Vultures," "Night Walk," "The Temporary World," & "Unfinished Landscapes"
Paterson Literary Review:	"On Hearing Word of her Death"
Philadelphia Poets:	"The Old Neighborhood"
Pittsburgh Quarterly Review:	"In the Portrait Gallery"
Plume:	"Anole," "The Coming Autumn" & "Rat"
Rye Whiskey Review:	"Here, Today"
Salamander:	"Wild Life"
Schuykill Valley Journal:	"Pet Sounds"
South Dakota Review:	"After Parting"

Vallum (Canada):	"When Lying was in Vogue"
Vox Populi:	"Grafton Street, St. Stephen's Green," "Security,"
	& "A Slight Misunderstanding"

The author would also like to thank the editors and publisher of several anthologies in which several of these poems appeared.

"Here Today" and "Pet Sounds" appeared in *Poet Sounds*. Christine Stroud and Gerry LaFemina, eds. City Lit Press.

"The First Church of the Long-Haul Trucker" appeared in *Endlessly Rocking: Poems in Honor of Walt Whitman's 200th Birthday*. Stan Galloway and Nicole Yurcaba, eds. Unbound Content.

"That Autumn Sunday" appeared in *Grabbed: Poets and Writers respond to Sexual Assault*. Elisa Albo, Richard Blanco, Caridad Moro, and Nikki Moustaki, eds. Beacon Press.

Gerry would like to thank the following: Jennifer Browne for the years of friendship and keeping the Frostburg literary community alive; my many writer friends: Gregg Wilhelm, Jan Beatty, Richard Blanco, George Guida, Lee Ann Roripaugh, Judith Vollmer, Lynn McGee, Jerry Wagoner, Madeleine Barnes, Susanna Case, Hilary Sideris, Michael Waters, Mihaela Moscaliuc, Christine Stroud, Nancy Mitchell, Jimmy Long, Phil Memmer, Marty Williams, Rick Campbell, Richard Peabody, Cornelius Eady, Linda Blaskey, Sherry Chappelle, Doug VanGundy, Elizabeth Savage, Allison Joseph, Phil Border, Bob Kunzinger, Jean O'Brien, Enda Wiley; the English Department of Frostburg State University for the support; Frostburg State University for a sabbatical that provided me with time to work on many of these poems; the MFA Program at Carlow University for the extended literary community; and most of all to my family, Mercedes Hettich, Alex LaFemina, Toni LaFemina, Mike and Barbara LaFemina, and Robyn and Owen Breslin for years of support.

CONTENTS

The End of Childhood . . . 9

One

When Lying Was in Vogue . . . 13
Daughters and Sisters of Charity . . . 15
In the Portrait Gallery . . . 17
Grafton Street, St. Stephen's Green . . . 19
Boa Constrictor . . . 20
The First Church of the Long-Haul Trucker . . . 21
Night Driving . . . 24
Approaching Equinox . . . 25
Buzzard . . . 27
Watching the News, I'm Reminded of the New York of Childhood . . . 28
After the War for Independence . . . 30
Porcupine . . . 32
Let the Evidence for the Divine be Found . . . 33
Unfinished Landscapes . . . 35
Almost . . . 37
Derecho . . . 40
Waking Early to Birdsong I Think of Our History of Loss . . . 41
The Old Neighborhood . . . 42
Rat . . . 44
The Last Farmer's Market of the Season . . . 45
The Far Pasture . . . 47
The Morning After We Push the Clocks Back . . . 49
That Autumn Sunday . . . 51

Two

Looking for Caravaggio . . . 55

Three

Kind of Blue . . . 61

Night Walk . . . 63

Wild Life . . . 65

Scenic Overlook, I-68 East, Maryland . . . 66

In Spring a Young Man's Fancy Turns . . . 68

Variation on the Third Law of Motion . . . 70

Raccoon . . . 71

The Asymmetry of Time . . . 72

The Coming Autumn . . . 75

Anole . . . 77

Approaching Thanksgiving . . . 78

Solstice . . . 80

On Hearing Word of her Death . . . 82

A Slight Misunderstanding . . . 84

Big Brown Bat . . . 86

It's Christmas. The turkey vultures. . . . 87

O Holy Night . . . 88

Up Early, I Turn off the Television News . . . 89

The Temporary World . . . 92

The Ever After . . . 94

Club Soda . . . 97

Dog . . . 99

Pet Sounds . . . 100

Here, Today . . . 101

Security . . . 103

Four

Sex & Death to the Age Fourteen . . . 107

I'll be the American poet
whose loneliness, finally, is relevant
whose slightest movement
ripples cross-country.

– Stephen Dunn

The End of Childhood

When the Cavern closed, that basement pet shop where I spent
after school afternoons
feeding the fresh waters & salt waters, &

told in hushed tones my small desires to the electus parrot
who knew my name—
when the Cavern closed for good years after

we'd left that neighborhood of wire trash cans & PTA mothers
in line at the deli
waiting for brown bag lunch specials on white

to be served with a baggie full of cookies, a can of Coke—
when the Cavern closed,
what did they do with the fish, two rooms

wall to wall of aquariums, each lit from above so the water
glowed fluorescent,
tank after tank of tetras, guppies, swordtails

or else the colorful & exotic Fancy Wrasses & Clown Triggers
some almost lighted
from within, as if gifted with a spark of creation

as if the Talmudic teachers were right, & purple blackcap basslets
(nothing like them
swam off Midland Beach: just jellyfish & whatever

lafayettes the old-timers caught, or else the crabs hauled in
in homemade traps).
Imagine trucks taking what couldn't be sold

when the Cavern closed to some other pet store, the fish
in giant plastic bags,
gills pulsing red & terrible as men in coveralls

carried each bag carefully because it was full of living creatures, &, too,
because they were paid
for their caution, had a reputation for it.

What of that bird in his coat of feathers suitable for Joseph,
squawking sometimes, still
calling my name—it was a word he knew after all—

squabbling as the men left & returned empty handed,
its head cocked
saying *Hullo! Hullo!*

When Lying Was in Vogue

Even laughter was a lie. Even sadness.
The way highways stretched beyond the next curve
with their markers every tenth of a mile &

their exit signs promising fuel & coffee,

the possibility of a bed with its vague suggestion
of desire. Nothing so tawdry. It was winter.
Snow didn't fall, so the road felt easy

but even our good fortune was a falsehood

had I been listening. By then
the politicians had embroidered their speeches
with so many fibs rehearsed so often

it wasn't difficult to believe &

America with its beaches & skyscrapers,
its trailer parks, its promise of equality,
its promise in the pursuit of happiness—

who didn't want to have faith? I carried mine

in my wallet like an ID card. Isn't that why
we traveled state by state & spoke of love &
ignored willfully every truth. We were, after all,

writers of fiction. Elsewhere people lied

in Portuguese, in Mandarin, in Pig Latin,
even in baby talk at the edge of strollers.
I knew my parents had lied often & for decades—

the fiction of that childhood with its televised

myths of the future all jet packs & the nuclear
family, might well have been an advertisement,
billboards lit up, suggesting some delicacy

for dinner everyone would enjoy.

We'd been duped before... In the Decoy Museum
placards told the storied history of wooden ducks,
of mallards, drakes, & teals, & how today

they're made by 3-D printers, the replicants

so precise you can see the veins on each feather.
Later, in the car, you laughed often,
the Cure on the radio—all lies

the way love songs always lie & are necessary.

This poem, too, which I conceived then. Remember,
there was an exhibit of sunken duck blinds,
how they'd been outlawed for the hunters would lay

submerged, shotguns ready, decoys buoyed above.

Oh, how beautiful I believed you were.
Every fifteen minutes church bells lied
about the time, about salvation.

Daughters and Sisters of Charity

Three nuns walked into the pub—
this isn't meant to have a punchline. They were there,
full habits, wimples, sensible shoes.
                                    The whole tavern went
contemplative but for the juke box which continued
Guns 'n' Roses. "Take Me Back to Paradise City."

What order were they—Carmelites? Sisters of Mercy?
They ordered margaritas. I thought of the Dominicans
who taught me, Sister Marcella & the two Marys:
Sister Mary Sourpuss & Sister Mary Playface—
none of whom I could imagine drinking tequila,

though once I saw them in street clothes at the mall,
jeans & nondescript sneakers, undercover nuns
until one of them called out to me. I was twelve,
thought only I was allowed a private life.
The rest of the afternoon I continued
                                    to look for them
paranoid I'd have to account for my trespasses,

the way in the bar the chatter had shrunk to classroom whisper
& the first *Goddamn* about a spilled manhattan
got followed by *Oh, shit. I'm so sorry.* It was hard to say
how old they were, & the bartender didn't ask for ID.
I was there as witness,
                        the whiskey was just
something I whispered my secrets to
so I could take them back, swallow them. Outside

the city's lovelorn walked the sidewalk squares trying
to believe again in the romance of urban solitude,
convincing themselves once more of its cool solace
while the criminal sect made hushed conspiracies
of broken windows & want,

of jail cell or confessional.
The doors of this place like a cathedral's. Those sisters drank

easily, maybe readying for a mission trip to Mexico
where Mezcal might be part of communion. Agave. Amen.
They murmured among themselves the way the three
who found the seal broken, the stone rolled away, must have
spoken to each other, a little spooked afterward
confused, muted,
                    which is how they left us all
when they rose after the second round, Rosary beads raining

briefly along the tabletop, & we remained that way
uncertain but not stunned. We never wondered what melancholy
they may have hidden in those robes. We'd seen so much already,
after all. How long had it been since any of us last sought penance?
Each of us with a penchant for spirits & whatever haunts us,
until forgetting becomes a way to forgive. Bar light haloing the lacquer.
Someone punched up
                    Leonard Cohen on the juke

for *there's a blaze of light in every word,*
it doesn't matter what we'd heard,
the holy or the broken hallelujah,
& we all raised our glasses of whatever liquor had been poured
each tumbler a momentarily held shard of stained glass.

In the Portrait Gallery

Faces of no one I know, some of them
stern-eyed, the rooms they sit in

soot-dark with coal fires & still births.
Thus was born stoicism & the Age of Exploration.

I lived that way for decades—
alternating between hermitage & pilgrimage.

the yin & yang of grim & grin.
Sure, the men in those paintings must have

waltzed at balls, fallen in love, laughed
despite a chronic, flaring abscess.

Absent biography, I can only guess their stories—
statesmen, husbands, slave holders, tycoons:

they all sit chisel-cheeked & upright.
Uptight. I know the young couple

rushing off for the stairwell, she leading, looking
over her shoulder, teeth light on her lip

in a way that is certainly about longing,
for I've been them, my young girlfriend

cooing, *Prove you love me.* How could I refuse
in that era when I'd confuse desire & eros?

Because theirs was the only happiness there
my eyes lingered until the doorway became another

frame on a portrait of a might-have-been life.
I'd like to mention the ecstasy of her

public touch, the waiting, the adrenaline &
endorphin crest, but really all I recall is how

I said her name, later that night,
when I should have been arrested

in revelry, victorious in our daring,
but instead I lay, lonely in my room,

bewildered & brooding while outside
raccoons ransacked the week's trash.

Grafton Street, St. Stephen's Green

Above the ruckus & din of Dublin—
busker song, busses muttering
in the insistent dialect of diesel,
tourists discussing wool & tweed,
whiskey & the Book of Kells—
church bells call out deliberately
the twelfth hour, thus reminding us
we're halfway between yesterday
& tomorrow, though after the first
toll we're closer to what's ahead,
whatever loss awaits. A young man
implores each of us for Euros
moving from stranger to stranger
with a story we've heard before—
a sick mother he needs to see
or else a daughter hungry at home.
So many imperatives on this street.
So many pigeons, chests puffed out
like footballers after a win.
All aluminum & glass, the streetcars
might well have been ordered from
some sci-fi utopia, & last week
I rode one past an 18th century
abbey & the squares of lost saints.
The woman five time zones west,
does she live in the country of the past
or of the future? We've counted
the passport stamps of heartache
& hope. The bells stop finally,
their last vibrations in a frequency
only angels can hear. Addressing them
by pet names, I quietly petition each
then take coins from a pocket. Tithe.

Boa Constrictor

Not asp, not cobra, not copperhead, diamond back, nor rattler.
Not one of those pythons left to grow large in the Everglades.

Not one of the snakes, too, St. Patrick banished into legend
from Ireland. No, it lay most days in a glass tank, impatient,

I bet, for night when it might slither up the branches & rocks
placed there for its amusement. Sometimes, sure, we'd reach in

lift it with two hands if only to scare our more squeamish friends.
Hadn't we been raised on stories of the serpent, the fruit,

& paradise, just another home we'd been asked to leave?
Not a garter or water moccasin, names like something

we might find in a closet. Not a cottonmouth or king.
I still remember its cool scales, heavy along my arms, the way

it unhinged its mouth to eat a mouse whole, & how when I left
for good, the wind hissed, flicking its tongue against my skin.

The First Church of the Long-Haul Trucker
for Jen Browne

I've crossed the bridge christened in your honor,
Walt Whitman, & pumped gas in your service plaza, too.
Where was I headed? What was I up to? No doubt

eros drove me to drive those drawn out highways cut through
cedar groves—one more erroneous decision. No doubt
the narrative isn't interesting enough for either of us.

Interstate light barely fingering the median foliage,
a familiar frustration. The man by the rest stop entrance
with his sign scrawled *Richmond*, his mosquito-netting beard,

his forlorn, water-marked fedora, how his hand twitched
in a manner that seemed bewitched, & how
I considered letting him ride beside me, if only to the state line,

though I don't regret leaving him behind—miles ago, years ago—
awaiting whatever trucker might have hauled him
deeper into these United States. The semi with its *oversize load*,

a cathedral-bound cross, gigantic, stainless,
a soon-to-be-steeple almost gleaming in the station lamps,
so heavy on its trailer it can't bear any more confessions.

If its driver is an agnostic, he only believes in mileage & home-
cooking. He must crush amphetamines into his coffee,
throw out the Bible tracts Christians offer. He's never read one

of your poems, Walt, not even in high school when he watched
the way the sun transformed basketball hoops into halos
for Saint No-one, & how May's maple leaves became silver dollars.

Maybe he imagined an older girl beneath those branches,
her back against the trunk bark, his mouth & hers, her hands
enmeshed in his hair. *Imagined...* He hasn't missed her in decades

can't even recall her name, remembers
only that she wrote poems, & how, hoping to impress her,
he checked out one of the library's four poetry titles.

He chose Frost—not Keats or Dickinson or you—
not that it made a difference. What is it about the past
that it seems to want to last, to linger into the present?

Walt, you understood the body & all its demands—
its sweat, toils, & passions. Its holy vigor. Somewhere
south of D.C. the First Church of the Long-Haul Trucker

offers respite & Bible study in an asphalt parking lot
all chrome & halogen. All prosperity gospel delivered
by a minister known for rigorous sermons. I've seen its billboards

the very way I've witnessed a semi shuddering to a halt
on a runaway truck ramp, tires smoldering.
I've shopped in the mall named in your honor, sat

in your Brooklyn park where I read someone your Calumas poems
& after the last line, she said she loved me & believed it,
needed to believe it, even. Conviction being integral to fidelity.

When that truck finally pulled out from the service station,
an advance vehicle led the way, its amber beacons swirling,
illuminating the fog; the dark cross,

obscured by the mist, borne southward
with all its promise for the next world. Who doesn't want
fulfillment in this one? I passed it

a few miles toward Delaware, alone in my car,
then passed the advance pick up, too, leading like a prophet
until even its twirling lights vanished

in the rearview. *Allons!*
To that which is endless as it was beginningless.
Allons! The road is before us.

Night Driving

Dark movements rimmed with light.
— Naomi Shihab Nye

Giant shadows of wind, the semis blow by,
bemoaning lost mileage; the drivers
on that mad combination of caffeine, adrenaline,
& speed. The skyline something crossed out—
not a bad word, necessarily, but a right phrase
at the wrong moment. Again
I wanted to say how like the night she is,
familiar, surprising, uncontainable.
The road to her is 314 miles long.
It unravels like a paragraph. My travelogue
is the story of how we met in a cursive
no one can decipher. It includes a litany
of curses in a tongue long forgotten.
Sometimes I tell her *I love you*, which is to say
I confuse her name with God's, particularly
when the last song on the radio is one
that always reminds her of an old crush.
States still separate us. My hands
on the steering wheel, its curve
like the curve of heaven, the arc of earth.
Ahead: the indulgent sadnesses of heartache.
Ahead: the flashing lights of cruiser & fire trucks,
some accident on a fast-approaching interchange.

Approaching Equinox

This afternoon I'm not interested in birds
but rather in how their shadows cross
the sidewalk in front of me, & in how

the laughter of playground kids resounds, sing-
song calls & responses reduced to syllables
& something resembling melody.

Thus, I can assume the season's first
ice cream trucks have come out of hibernation.
I'd like one of those swirled cones

so I might consume non-duality,
lick it from my fingertips even
in a way my mother would reprimand.

There's a reason someone invented napkins.
There's a reason, too, for motorcycles—
these first days of brilliance & warmth, though

only the doppler complaint of a sport exhaust
let's me know they're out there, driving off:
late model Harleys, Triumphs. Tomorrow the equinox,

but the weatherman divines a last cold front
heading our way, so don't put away those parkas,
those gloves & scarves just yet.

There are moments she says she loves me
as casually as throwing a shadow;
other times it's as if her tongue were

a patchwork of beaks & feathers,
Isn't this how it's always been?
Gratitude is, the primatologist claims,

a universal animal emotion. Ditto hurt.
Ditto affection. Of all the great apes,
only humans mate for the long term

at least on paper. That couple who hurried past,
hands held, must have been picking up
their kids from the park, then they'll stop

for soft serve & shakes on the way home.
It's so American, isn't it,, the scene
almost staged by an ad agency. As if in on it,

the sun winks in all the storefront windows.
Sure, I've been a sucker before:
I've banged my fists against my chest,

declaring my devotion. A little after six,
shadows stretch toward the East River,
& happy hour patrons join me on Seventh Ave.

When the wind gusts harder, we're all
reminded it's still winter. It's clear
by how pigeons tuck their heads against the clamor.

Buzzard

That's no buzz cut: the bird's totally bald
in its black cassock like a defrocked friar,
watching, always watching

from the tree some twenty yards away.
What Friday carrion does its breath reek of?
What disease must it carry in its beak?

See how much it looks like
the goth kids I once knew so well, sullen,
all dark clothes & pale skin,

their talk of vampires or dying
or desire. Our hungers reminded us
we were alive after all, despite

the vultures inside our chests vibrating
their wings against cages of bone,
wanting to either fly off or feast.

Watching the News, I'm Reminded of the New York of Childhood

Today's footage of Kabul highlights rubble & cars
on fire; children begging chocolates from G.I.s. Yesterday

it showed poppy fields & Afghan men with Kalashnikovs
following Humvees with their eyes, the way

addicts watched passing squad cars—
the Lower East Side in the decade of decay, our streets

mostly cobble & potholes. Testimony of wannabe prophets
hieroglyphed in neon spray on the D train, the whole city

seeming to anticipate the blackout, the Son of Sam, punk rock.
Junkies nodded out on tenement steps,

almost inconceivable these days when former porn houses
host 100 dollar-a-ticket dramas.

No one masturbates in *those* bathrooms, for now
nearly everyone mutes their longing. Squatters used to stay

in an Avenue A walk-up right by my aunt's apartment.
Stolen wire unspooled, stretched from a streetlamp

through a fractured window. Guardian Angels & kabbalists
walking in opposite direction without acknowledgment.

Black Panthers & Hare Krishnas, too. Sirens
hot-rodding to the latest inferno—a Chevy Impala

ablaze by the curb. The stickball kids just moved
one block over, boom boxes tuned to disco stereo.

How easy it was to feel marooned on the stoop.
The looming decade would be all Kangol caps,

crack, & AIDS as reported by cable television.
The Soviets would invade Afghanistan, & Reagan

would pin a flag to his lapel—how so many cheered, &
soon we'd learn a vocabulary that included *mujahedeen*.

The mayor promised the sanitation men would return,
so the trash piled high on sidewalks would be hauled away.

Despite the humidity July wore like a shawl,
the lingering pungency dissipated, & the flies

that had grown fat among bags of chicken bones & sour milk
flew off, the maggots carried to the landfill. Whatever

remained was washed toward the sewers
when the city opened fire hydrants those scorched days.

Somewhere there's a Polaroid of a young boy,
nearly naked, eating a stolen Hershey bar in the spray.

After the War for Independence

Those boys in the basement, middle-school aged, unruly
Kiss pinballing among the wood panels—*Destroyer*—,
scent of model glue & some stepmother's menthols
heavy in the already heavy air. No A/C.
The fifth of July. Five of us at a table

unravelling duds & unspent bottle rockets
collecting silver powder on paper sheets, shaking it
into larger & larger stockpiles beside stolen
rolling paper. We'd pick up each unused fuse,
measure its length. The seventies, the five boroughs

seemed so close to detonation, the whole country.
We were mesmerized by destruction on tv,
on the streets, on movie screens in the cinemas
we snuck into, the films rated R for nudity,
language, & violence. We were all braggadocio.

This was the adult world we were prepping for,
so why wouldn't we strive to make a bigger bang,
something louder, like a forgotten villain,
harbinger of chaos & laughter. The rest couldn't know
one of us would blow up a pay phone hoping for

a cavalcade of dimes, & *he* couldn't know just then,
as the lit fuse dwindled toward detonation,
a woman would need to make a call.
Was it the concussion that made our windows tremble?
This wasn't Belfast or London. Not Beirut or Tel Aviv.

The only Troubles we knew were the ones we sought
or else found in electric guitar squeal & bursts of percussion.
There was no ideology beyond boredom & curiosity,
beyond nameless frustration. In the discussions later
he lacked remorse, asserted only that she'd been unlucky

—wrong place, wrong time, as if my friend were a sudden
acolyte of fate, some accursed angel. If I remained silent
it was because I was culpable, because I was lonely
& knew not to snitch, because I realized such a news story
might be pushed back to page three when a body was found,

headless, with no ID in a dumpster. But I couldn't know that
except in hindsight. Face facts: we were thirteen,
incapable of perceiving anyone's pain but our own,
which was existential & without words. All that night
I used the abacus of a Rosary to tally up my sins,

sum up my years to come in Purgatory. The smell outside
all sulphur & brimstone when the sun finally burned
the haze away. How the asphalt almost melted; it glowed
watery in the distance like a mirage. The beat cops
talked to so many in the neighborhood for a few days.

One said he was listening to every lead. Another,
that the woman lost an ear, her face scalded & scarred.
Someone said he picked up from the other side of the police tape
fifteen dollars in change. That was the last time we spoke
though I'd continue to give him a nod when we passed

or between classes because that's how conspirators work.
How cool that basement was, though I refused to go back,
choosing to sweat in front of Wile E. Coyote's explosions.
The Road Runner always fast enough. When the phone rang
I wouldn't answer it, just let it jingle in the empty kitchen.

Porcupine

Oh, we envied their quills, stuck out

perfect defense for the slam dance pits

we preferred. They're quiet, too

shuffling out onto highways only

on occasion. Tough & shy

we knew them, dark eyes hunting

food or companionship. We knew them:

their musk, the gods they worshiped,

the hymns they listened to

all windsweep & thunder.

Let the Evidence for the Divine be Found

Sudden storm burst—rush of rain round & large
snapping asunder against the windshield; like
popcorn kernels opening in surprise, each
in succession, the drops blossom then fade out
in a moment, fluid blooms we can't see

but might insist are beautiful, & look, we're right,
we realize, in the time lapse photographs of
a hurricane—freeze-framed watery flowerets, translucent,
reflecting what little light available, spark
of the ineffable filling each. The rabbi

stands at the temple door watching this deluge,
wondering, yet again, not about the covenant
between God & man, but about what Ezekiel saw,
that fiery wheel, those horrific figures. We spoke about them
at the bar after another disappointing Mets game,

one with an hour-long rain delay, the tarp unspooled
to cover the base paths. It was supposed to be
Fireworks Night, but the tempest cancelled all those
rocket launches, so no flashing spirals swirled
above the stadium. Instead we discussed Rilke's angels,

which are terrifying every one of them, voices like thunder—
triumphant yet devastating, shaking the walls no doubt
until car alarms echo through the parking lot.
Ambulance clarion. Sound rising to efflorescence then
falling off, so much like love with the praise to God,

always with the seventies cliche sparklers bursting
in the sky at each kiss. Then it's finished,
the rain over as quickly as it arrived. Thus, umbrellas wilt
& fold. Thus, my friend finally leaves the synagogue
to do his good deeds at Beth Israel, its fluorescent lit

corridors among the suffering & machines, hospital gowns
gauzy as angel wear. Sometimes it's as if the Lord's forsaken
those rooms. I remember shuddering when the elevator
opened onto the children's ward, Sloane Kettering, &
a different elevator in a rehab clinic where I arrived with gladiolas

& for the last time. How the light was the same
harsh white. A woman I slept with there, how she used
to load her syringes, tighten a tourniquet,
then depress the plunger gently to remove any air, though
sometimes a drop or two of junk might push out, &

such was her addiction she would whimper in
the language of terror, a language undecipherable, a cry that
rose, unfolding until I couldn't bear it, & turned away even
as it relaxed into decrescendo. Out the window street lamps
filled the puddles, brilliant shivering florets on damp asphalt.

Unfinished Landscapes

My friend Peter pointed out the condensation
on his glass & declared how much love is like water:
everyone wants it, & how it comes

in a torrent or a trickle, though it can also be
a still pond with mosquitos, cirrus-like, above it
so that sometimes we might confuse

the soft insect buzz for love itself, but no.
The water metaphor was what was important
in the end—how we thirst & how

we can't cup it in our hands for it seeps
between fingers as we bring it to our mouths
so it's as if we kiss our own palms.

Some people, in desperation, get on their knees
bend over like a dog to lick at a puddle.
So easily we lose our dignity, & easily, too,

we fight for it or weep in its name.
That's something never taught in science class.
Ditto how to cope with heartache or how to enjoy

the way sunlight seems to cast itself
on only select leaves of a spring catalpa
so they grow a little greener, more lush & thus

more lovely. Ask the landscape artist I see some days
in May, in Central Park, & he'll show you how
he mixes acrylics, shade after shade of emerald

whisked in, sometimes, a bit of yellow to nix
a daub of blue, then feeling it thinned out too much
adding something darker. The brush swirling in hues

so that it resembles a smeared thumb print,
a bit of forensic evidence, the way the fine brush hairs
form thin ridges in the paint.

Then it, too, is gone. Likewise, day's luminescence
which gives way to evening with a shuffling sound
that can only be described as wind through leaves.

The painter picks up his tubes, canvas, & easel
though he'll stop to let you know that
this is another in a series of unfinished landscapes, &

that he used to paint boaters on the lake
from one of the stone bridges.
It made him hopeful, somewhat nostalgic—

those couples with their secret languages &
picnic baskets, their laughter
competing with busker song & the giddiness of kids

clutching balloon strings. He never says what changed
his mind, or how much sadness is like sunlight—
ubiquitous, momentary. Along the curving path

comes a woman with a poodle, whistling
Tchaikovsky's *Rites of Spring*. There's no call for rain,
yet an umbrella swings from her free hand.

Peter would say that proves everything.

Almost

Sky the shade of dark washed denim,
first stars riveted in place, seeming to hold the galaxy together.
Maybe that's why cosmologists talk about
                                                    the fabric of spacetime.

If I once placed all my chips on desire & then watched
the wheel as it spun to see where the ball dropped,
it wasn't about fulfillment but about possibility—

the body's insuppressible urges
                                        no touch can purge.
How she might say my name or finger
my arm casually,
                in that manner that says *I know this man,*
his whims and follies, his promise and faults. So what
he falls in love so easily?

Why were there nights when I'd leave that room
believing she slept
                                & pour myself a small amount of bourbon
just to enjoy the color & scent of it
before looking out the window into the night-lit yard

where a skunk or racoon slunk the perimeter.
Bats I couldn't see circling above the apple tree, hungry for insects.

When I crept back to that room, crept
because I didn't want to hurt her feelings with my absence
I'd pause to stare not at her face pressed against the pillow,
her mouth that I had watched, teeth clenched through orgasm, now slack

nor at the way her body made contours of the comforter,
but at the shed jeans on the floor,
                                a specter of hours earlier.

I even touched them with my bare toes
as if I wanted to return to longing
right before she'd pat the space beside her summoning me back.

We strolled neighborhood streets & said little of consequence

our voices like that of mosquitoes humming in amorphous clouds
though sometimes there was a thunderclap of laughter;

how she wrote *to-do* lists on napkins with *kiss you*
always the lead.
                    Wanting and wanting more what defined us.

Isn't that what consumerism teaches?
Even the teens in *Defy Authority* t-shirts, who walk the mall
practicing their flirtations, understand this.

If the past casts its filmy shadow
so the sun seems stalled at the horizon, how can we talk
about the temporality of it all? Even

the scabbed bumps of insect bites will pass
though they itch & burn.
                              Though we scratch till bloody.
She used to watch documentaries about the universe's beginning,
about the way galaxies revolved
                              around super massive black holes.

She could name the constellations.
I liked that. Liked, too, how she looked at me,
                                        which was almost enough.
She knew myths, believed aliens were models
for our old gods. She only shrugged
when I asked where they'd gone. New quantum equations suggest

the universe has no origin: no big bang, no genesis.
Despite talk of making memories,

I have no photographs
of us together, not on some early date, our expressions
all excitement & wonder.

There was one night, though, when I hadn't left the bed
when we stirred by the neighbor's failed service dog
baying for five minutes.
                                    Followed by quiet.

How alarmed he'd sounded. How forlorn.
We lay awake for an hour afterward, our bodies nearly touching,
both aware of the distance there,
                                    the few inches between us.

After breakfast sunlight startling the grain of the hardwood floors
I watched her feet, then calves, then thighs
slide into her indigo jeans
                                    & felt a brand-new sense of futility.

When I reached to touch her, she gently swatted my hand away.
What power in the word *later*.

It's only us who understand impermanence.

She left,
            her coffee cup half full on the nightstand, &
shut the door so gently so as to not ripple what remained;
I don't know how she did it,
but that dog didn't even whimper as she walked past its fence.

Derecho

The wind, as if in heat, knocks
at the windows. So much hunger even
on this cul-de-sac with its full
garbage cans & buzz-cut lawns. Street-
lights blush but keep staring. A whole
community of voyeurs & exhibitionists,
the church prudes with their gossip,
coffee, & pastries after gospel
lessons from the pulpit. The storm
remembers the old prayers, too,
those pleas for intervention; it bears
the answers in dust & leaves,
mini cyclones of debris.
An electric aftertaste that lingers.
All this love & lust. All this
lonesomeness. First days after
the Feast of Saints, the Feast of Souls,
yet still a few weeks from bounty.
If God is a vengeful god let him
come when we call his name,
shuddering. Shutters bang
in the gale, magnolia branches
rattle the panes so we're afraid
for a moment that the glass &
the moment behind it, might shatter.

Waking Early to Birdsong I Think of Our History of Loss

Predawn sparrows aflutter, *chirrup*
chirrup, under the awning by my window, &

the littler cat already by the glass cracking
the knuckles of both paws,
as if dreaming of feathers & marrow. How

Mao Zedong ordered their killing—one of four pests
to be eradicated. The Great Leap Forward.

Thus 1958 was filled with gunfire &

the beating of drums, so the birds, too frightened
to land, fell from the air
                          exhausted, literally

dropping dead.

Another day advances into the vacant rooms
illuminates the artifacts of what I've almost forgotten,

their shrouds of dust & loss.
                          The cat only knows appetite.
Consider this: no one foresaw the consequences:

the plague of insects in '59, the famine, the lack of cheer
in the daily lives of villagers who couldn't say

what was missing come early spring mornings,

those bright sharp notes, the way
each bird had seemed to carry lightspark in its beak.

The Old Neighborhood

If it weren't for the chain-link it would be
easy to overlook, weeds overwhelming

the infield, even the base paths overgrown,
dirt now seeded, pitching mound flattened,

the whole diamond rutted—so many
potential sprained ankles. Decades abandoned,

the dugout benches sag, pine soggy with rot.
Like my uncles, the boys who once played here

became men who spend nights watching the Orioles
on television. Cynthia's Tavern. Beers cold & watery,

cheap as old aspirations. The bar used to sponsor
a softball team but not since Pat Benatar

warned how love is a battlefield. So prescient.
Pub glasses suffer night sweats. The tales told there

almost redundant: another woman, another man,
a lie told not to hurt someone, the way so many

lies cover sharper truths. Their sons never
played catch, never joined pick-up games or

Little League; instead they learned soccer & video
basketball, stopped listening to stories

that start in the bottom of the ninth, of pennants
lost by sacrifices or diving catches; they don't care

about bleacher seat foul balls nearly caught
or extra innings on tiny black and white screens.

Those sons have left home. They rarely call, much
less return with grandsons. How the fathers envy them &

thus sit with their sullenness & their bottles peeled
of labels. Beyond the forgotten outfield, rabbits hide

among the brambles & grasses, snakes skimmer:
remember how such things would have excited them once?

On the bar mantle, the little metal batters of trophies,
always ready for a fastball down the pipe,

swing only at dust. Who said hell is for children?
As penance, no one's forced to write

apologies to old coaches, & that former shortstop
who became a judge has never sentenced

reform school dropouts to return the field
to playability. A lightning storm shakes the windows,

a heavy branch breaks from a sudden strike,
the jagged crash like the crack of a home run bat,

a bright inning in a losing game. It seemed
to rain like this often then, one of them says.

Those were some storms. No one disagrees.

Rat

The albino one Rachel owned looked
so much like her— thin, elongated face,

coarse white hair, skin pink, & the teeth . . .
her smile, alluringly feral. These nights,

when winter skitters around the houses, &
snow teases the black leather crowd

I hear her laughing all joy & cruelty
—the way she did always before we kissed.

The Last Farmer's Market of the Season
—in memoriam, Jon Tribble & Kim Shattuck

The news comes as it does these days in waves
across tiny screens—a text message followed
by Facebook tributes, the unmediated
social media of consolation & grief.
No hoarse voices. No sobbing on the phone's
other end. Some post acronyms. Platitudes
instead of disbelief's silence. Two friends
in a few hours in two different cities
in this country where the interstates seem
suddenly longer, as if miles had become
leagues. Already darkness stretches
its quilt across the Appalachian sky,
but in Carbondale & in Los Angeles
the sun still does it what it does
brilliantly & without respect for widows
& widowers. October. The talk's all
skeletons & ghosts, but there's nothing spooky
about death, not at all. It comes. We grieve.
When we wake the morning windows
are no different in their indifference.
Ditto the dogs who wag their tails for water
& kibble. The bereaved just pick through
their closets, put on our clothes because
what other choice do we have? Later,
evening will return because it's unending
& it will be someone else's turn
to gasp, to weep, that's the mechanics of it,
the relentlessness of melancholy, of keening,
the line of mourners in black outfits
outside the funeral home. Their laughter
shocking & heavy as a heron lifting off.
Tomorrow we get dressed, we go
to work with that ache in an attaché case
or purse, a small curse, like a bad taste,

we're afraid to utter, afraid of what
it might do out there, dispersed
among others. Phone in hand a young kid
strolls by singing in a not-so-good voice,
& we consider how fortunate, privileged even,
to be able to hear him, even as his notes
falter. Each of his breaths a condensation puff
evaporating while at the farmer's market
the first vendors set up their stalls
with what they've gathered from final harvests—
spicy peppers, plump tomatoes, those greens.

The Far Pasture

for Joseph Fasano

We had to shoot the horse—there was no other choice
but we did it humanely, we told ourselves
despite its pain: one high-caliber slug
through the brain case. An act
brutal & commonplace & necessary,
though I continue to hear the echo of the shot,
a slight, perpetual hum in the right ear, &
can't forget the splatter of bone fragment, blood, &
grey matter, so many hues of viscera followed
by the glossy blackness of crows. Even today I shiver

when I hear the concussion of fireworks.
The woman I was with then used to visit the stables often
to touch the sturdy flanks of stallions
as if the muscles under the hide could steady her.
She never received the palomino her parents had promised
so settled for the ones others kept
horses with names like Columbia's Monarch, Blazer Glory,
Dum Dum, names both hyperbolic & ill-suited she insisted.
Still, she stayed devoted to them,
sometimes sneaking among the stalls to talk to one or the other
nights the old fears returned

because the deep brown of a horse's eye,
the swell of it like a Buddha's belly, could be called compassion
if they made a crayon that rich & luscious.
Nights when her crying would wake me
I understood for the first time the words
inconsolable & futility & fidelity, which would be terrible names
for both colors & horses,
even the palest mare, the shade of the weak moon
rickety as a hansome cab making its way westward.

When I finally washed the sulfurous scent from my fingers,
when I no longer had a faith in a god of kindness,
I went out to the pasture
where a few yearlings grazed freely. In the distance
poplar trees swayed at a gallop.
Beyond them, even though I couldn't see her, I now know
that woman walked, making a decision
she insisted had nothing to do with me,
her hands on the strap of her bag as if gripping a bridle,
white, tight knuckled.
From the stable I heard a loud whinny,
which sounded either like laughter or weeping, I couldn't decide,
& then the wind chimes she'd hung on our porch
or else that ever present tinkling in my ear.

The Morning After We Push the Clocks Back

Rain like keystrokes on a typewriter, but no,
it's on the awning outside the living room though it hits, too,
the wet lawn with soft almost-splashes.
When I think of it, I imagine they shatter in little flashes of refracted
light, each droplet exploding beautifully.
The newsprint air obscures the white duplex across the street.
Rain on the final magnolia leaves, & then
one more leaf on the grass. No doubt the soundtrack
for this scene would be sad, cue
the minor key. Everything in stasis. Even the cats sleep in,
the soft motors of their bodies apurr,
fur rippling. Even my neighbors who ordinarily would
have released their dogs to bark their
furious, high-pitched alarm clock barks by now. Rain
in the expanding puddles—the world
outside straight from an art-house movie, one the critics call
atmospheric for its cinematography
& for its score, those mid-tempo harpsichord strikes,
each note a splash of sound, dizzyingly
simple in its phrasing. Not a storm. Not a drizzle. One of
those middle-management rains,
persistent & not-going-anywhere until the layoffs come.
We're past the era of paperboys.
The early morning joggers have all decided to take the AM off.
Can't say I blame them. The coffee steams.
A different me might've written about the cleansing
nature of precipitation, calling it
a baptism, but it's too early for church bell sermons, &
let's face it, some mornings even hope
seems overrated, especially for someone like me. No thunder.
No torrent. No crack in the cumulonimbus

hinting at daybreak. No car-sound
from the National Highway though the cats still growl through
their dreams. There's no movie I want to watch.
Just rain. Rain falling on the potholes the city left untaken care of.
Rain rattling itself along the walkway.
I don't need a weatherman to tell me it'll be like this all day.

That Autumn Sunday

The weeds genuflected all around the clearing
as if a sacrifice had to be given, &

the man with the knife
the man who zipped up, laughed

in a way some might be tempted
to over dramatize, &

turned away, so the wind that remained
seemed to tsk its tongue as if to shame

until even the sun
lowered its brilliant head.

Looking for Caravaggio

I'm looking for Caravaggio on side streets & alleys,
beside the stairwells to basement taverns
where drunkards brag & junkies settle
their debts by making fresh bets on past hopes—someone sells
secondhand magazines & records, someone else hawks
acrylic reproductions, each one a gambler making odds.

I'm looking for Caravaggio in that portrait of David,
there in the lovelorn & horrified eyes,
in the grimace & forlorn locks of Goliath's head
gripped in the slingshot boy's stony fist, which seems
to quiver with the play of shadow & light.

I'm looking for Caravaggio in D.C., in the National Gallery
among the Titians, Bellinis, & Giorgiones,
but there are none, the docent, like a disappointing nonna, says,
because they were precious or risqué
so out of fashion when the collection was conceived.

I'm looking for Caravaggio for he was
always a risky character, rascal, thug, the first punk.
Here, not so far from The Lute Players in Manhattan,
an electric guitar diluted with distortion
buzzes across the mall. A woman I love among the Impressionists,
but I've little desire for Parisian parks, no

I'm looking for Caravaggio because I'm longing
for a lost self, something
I miss in the mirror's reverse image,
that waggish adolescent thrown out of St. Peter's halls—

I'm looking for Caravaggio where I first saw him,
in that family Bible in the living room with its red cloth cover,
its ribbon tongues calling forth certain psalms,
twenty homes ago: the full color photograph

capturing Simon Peter's martyrdom, the old man
back against wood about to be
                                    crucified face down
although in the painting the soldiers haven't given up the hammer,
haven't, yet, lifted the cross fully.
Was that saint looking at the nail in his left wrist or at me

looking for Caravaggio in the chiaroscuro, those figures
looming from shadow & into the dark moments of their lives
as in the smoky clubs where I licked up whiskey & sweat,
promises & deceits, those things the gypsy girls
only blushed about & looked away when telling fortunes.

I'm looking for Caravaggio as Longhi had
before me, as Sir Dennis Mahon had,
as Pietrangeli, Correale, Cavesi, & Bigetti had,
as Francesca Cappelletti & Laura Testa had in musky archives
among family inventories & baroque ledgers,
mildew staining fading ink, the ancient illegible script.

I'm looking for Caravaggio in another National Gallery
that canvas of Judas just after he's kissed Christ.
Betrayal so often looks like this—so beautiful, so brutal,
a woman behind Jesus shrieking.
                                How amazing this canvas
found in a Jesuit sitting room misascribed to a German
with the very name my mother gave me. Is that him holding the lantern,
human Lucifer literally bringing the light?

I'm looking for Caravaggio in my palm, in my lifeline & love line,
in the lines of old poems & on subway lines
where tarot readers & tough guys both stare me down,
index fingers outstretched as if to dare.

I'm looking for Caravaggio as young sick Bacchus,
or is it me, lovesick, teen-aged, thirsty for more
the way I always seemed to be

as if the only way to satisfy desire was with more desire.
Where are either of them now? Dust & ether. Buzz of neon.

I'm looking for Caravaggio, & there he stands behind the dying
St. Ursula, none other than courtesan Lena he'd painted from memory.
How he must have missed her in the end.
How he strived to make the harlots holy
over & over, male & female lovers both,
how he knew every martyr has a body & every body wants.

I'm looking for Caravaggio, just one painting,
framed, enclosed like a confessional
where I might whisper my trespasses, the ones never committed
or committed to until uttered. Father's tattered breath
commuting a sentence:
                                 No Hail Marys. No Acts of Contrition.
Strange faces on the walk home half lit by windows & streetlamps.

I'm looking for Caravaggio in the curses & fights,
in the weeping, too, of autobiography, & in the way
she looked at me long after the museum closed that day,
after we'd drifted among grifters & addicts,
after we'd given some greenbacks to the corner psychic
who'd made no promises & so was like any of us,
& just minutes after she'd called to Jesus as we sinned
not for the first nor for the last time
in that capital city of apostles & apostates.

Kind of Blue

There is no time of day when no one else is awake,
so somebody must also be watching
the sky perform its singular magic trick, transforming itself

into daylight once again, channeling through
innumerable shades of blue that have
no Pantone designation, though I can imagine

one of the painters I know trying again to mix
the shade of 5:54 A.M. on December 10,
2015 above Cumberland, Maryland. Failing. Darkness

fading like a bruise, like the taste of coffee, like devotion,
even, yet sticking around. It's still too early
for the first joggers, & the one cop on duty clocks only wind

on his radar gun. In a few more minutes a waitress will
unlock the door of our town's sole diner, flip
the sign in the window from closed. The common ceremonies

of capitalism & community already at work
despite being too early for church bells,
& isn't that why we're glad to live in these States—something

so ordinary, so quotidian. For years I've forgotten
to be grateful for my right to complain,
to resist, & for the moon, which has already faded into obscurity

despite being so large it's kept meteors away. How fortunate
we are even to have evolved—astronomers
call this the Goldilocks Zone, the perfect distance from the sun

& from Jupiter, enough heat & light. A scientific miracle.
Just right. The sound of Miles Davis's trumpet
filling the rooms with warmth. This morning I mix oatmeal

balancing boiling water, milk, brown sugar. A chemist
studying conductivity discovered a new shade
of blue: how do you explain finding what must have always existed,

lost among a jay's plumage or at 5:57 A.M., slightly
to the northwest. All the great discoveries, after all,
have always been around. Ask Columbus. Ask the First Nations.

That moment I discovered I loved a woman because she was
alight in laughter & said something witty & insightful
about Russell Edson's work, the light through the window certain

in a way I'd never seen, ephemeral as a held note. Listening
to Miles & Coltrane together it's easy to have faith
in American exceptionalism, a notion with quaint nostalgia

like recalling an ex-lover or unwrapping Christmas
ornaments kept from childhood. Other days
I go to that diner, amazed by how many of us are there so early,

each in our own booth. The waitresses startlingly
alert, perky even, as the regulars flirt &
cup their coffee cups between both hands, breathing in the steam,

just right after morning's solitude & wind. Dawn coming
on its own sweet time, how I'll flip through the table's juke box songs,
seeking the hits of adolescence, ones I never choose to play.

Night Walk

Three bats scrape the undercarriage of dusk,
circle concentrically then swoop for summer's
remaining insects. They are scraps of darkness
against the darkening sky, the way certain notes
in a nocturne's melody resonate more,
cables vibrating from hammer strikes, sustained
almost a visible shiver, even as being played
by an unknown neighbor. E minor. Chopin.
The whole thing unsteady, uncertain, almost
unrecognizable, like the self in distant memory. Smoke
from a leaf fire a worn scarf against windsweep.
I didn't use to believe in ghosts despite a childhood
watching Chiller films Saturdays past midnight.
I didn't believe in mad scientists & undead.
Then I learned about the Bomb in class,
imagined being trapped in a basement shelter
with girls I had no courage to speak with
outside fantasy; the yellow & black fallout signs
that were everywhere it seemed, announced the inevitable.
Yet here we are nearly 40 years later, in Appalachia,
in an America that continues to advertise
custard cones, holiday parades, & Elvis impersonators
appearing at Autumn Glory band shells. For years
people kept seeing the King or his ghost—
the past unrelenting. Its soundtrack all nocturnes &
"Return to Sender," the occasional riff of swing
or bebop. The junior high kids, instead, fall in love
on the school bus or in Math class or during
active shooter drills, teacher saying any one of you
might be a victim, so follow directions. This is the way
we learn heartache, how even a name can be haunted
because a name can be a house we live in for years
walking in the empty rooms of its syllables.
We open the windows just to hear the beloved
breathing until that breath becomes the very back-beat

of our evenings. The properties of heartbreak & loss
all so similar, their overgrown lawns, their one lit rooms
behind curtains, envelopes uncollected in mailboxes.
No one knows what happened, though kids walking past
invent narratives, each one more horrific until
all that remains are the rumors themselves—
the plots like that of thrillers, all sadness or else
the threat of tragedy, & even this is American.
The piano appears again, this time Gershwin, more
furtive, further away. A feral cat rushes from wild fescue
a field mouse, metronomic tail swinging, clamped
in its fangs. Years ago, this might have been an omen.
To the distant west strobe lightning flashes without thunder.

Wild Life

The city warns that coyote have been sighted
broaching a few neighbors' yards. Scat & paw prints
discovered come dawn. They must be hungry &

desperate, trembling in the shadows beyond
the back porch, the way a secret lover once arrived
on summer nights. How much excitement in that

romance, right there next door to the gossipy so-and-so
with her wannabe perfect lawn, her *Jesus loves you*
bumper sticker. The moon like a lit lamp

through a curtained window. I hear yowls
in the wind or else it's the echo of radio song,
some crooner with his torch, his inevitable

hurt. The coyotes may be in heat—it's March
after all, so food & love have been scarce for months.
The motion light floods the yard momentarily.

The apple branches shiver in winter's last gusts
like a pilgrim. No one & nothing approaches
my porch anymore. Relentless & close

something yips—systolic-diastolic—well toward dawn.

Scenic Overlook, I-68 East, Maryland

The first greens of March still
weeks away, today is grey
sky over grey landscapes cut
by greyer roads with a gambler's
chance of disinterested rain.
To the south Virginia & West
Virginia though who can tell
them apart from this distance?
There's no line I can see, no
border other than some sign
saying *Welcome to...* or *Now leaving....*
Over the weekend breaking news
featured a girl found at the bottom
of this cliff face. Broken bones.
Lacerations. Her boyfriend dead.
A suicide pact, she insisted
from her hospital bed. The state
police closed this place for days,
red cones & lit signs telling us
though some gawkers parked
in the exit lane, hazards blinking,
& walked right in. Some noted
anomalies & inconsistencies &
suspected foul play. Where was
his car, after all? How did they
get this far without notice?
A dumb friend sworn silent
or an out-of-state driver who'd
stopped for two young hitchhikers?
Others speculated a *West Side Story*
situation—star-crossed paramours
that had finally said enough.
Something about opioids.
Something about meth. What
will happen to that girl? She's

the age of my students, who seem,
often, infatuated & sullen both.
Too late, our delegates debate
erecting a fence to prevent
anyone else from climbing over
the waist-high barricade, but that
would ruin the view. It's
breathtaking after all, the horizon,
if you can believe it, stretching out
on bright days to North Carolina.
Maybe it's possible in June
when the good green fills the leaves
& the valley, & the mountain sides
are sixty shades of vibrant. It's
a lucky thing, the news had said,
they'd jumped in January for
their dark figures were visible
against another snowfall. Come
verdant spring those bodies might
have been lost among the brush,
the lush overgrown undergrowth,
food for coyotes & carrion birds, so
it would seem like they'd just gone
from here as so many young people,
looking to escape, hoping
to take highways at 70 into
the myth of opportunity: sun lit
places just beyond Appalachian
mists so thick some mornings
they shroud everything, even
a mother's grief & bent shoulders,
even these remaining groves
of centuries old white oak.

In Spring a Young Man's Fancy Turns

The green slope flecked with yellow
dandelion, how picturesque, the way

those weeds almost collect spring light.
Remember, you gathered a bouquet of them

in your first-grade fist,
a gift for that freckled classmate whose name

you've surrendered, but not
how she kept them in a plastic cup water-filled

at her desk. After lessons
she rubbed the face of one under your chin

to see how rich you'd be.
How lemony did your skin become? You couldn't see,

but when her fingers
brushed against your cheek, you blushed so.

That flower-sized blemish
remained 'til bedtime, a misshapen kiss,

a pale hickey. The riches
promised, the treasure—how you imagined

in that small room you shared
with your brother, gold coins overflowing

the pockets of not-hand-me-downs,
because then you didn't know the difference

between fortune & good fortune
or between the sounds your neighbor made,

muffled moans from the other side of the wall:
who's to say, the wails of orgasm or of despair.

Variation on the Third Law of Motion

Some say David Hume is still relevant, others
talk Newton, especially in my neighborhood,
especially when a fire engine sings its solitary note
on Main Street and thus sets the first Shitzhou barking.
Then, down the block, a Malamut chimes in,
followed, further away, by a German Shepherd,
a cascade of barking with a few elongated howls
as if in imitation of the alarm. The cat in the window
jumps down. You stutter alert, ask what's wrong.
There's a hurricane delivering a series of body blows
in the Bahamas & farmers in the Midwest
sit in diners discussing soybeans slowly growing
moldy in silos. It was only a fire engine,
some emergency somewhere far from the refugee
camps, from ISIS safe houses where conspiracies
are being shaped, plans made, far from the crying
girl with the black eye, from the pillow-hidden pistol.
Our neighbor is telling her dog to behave,
to quiet down. Everything we know about heartache
in the tremor of her voice. The evidence suggests
you're done with sleep—it's in the restless pulse,
the cat now seeking solace beside you. The mailman
will deliver requests from the Food Bank & Red Cross,
from St. Jude's & the Wounded Warriors. Like a storm
surge need overwhelms, it's what directs the does
to the backyard—they're out there now—
despite the dogs barking, despite the traffic.
In their want they come for the windfall apples
that lie among the grasses, waiting to be grazed.

Raccoon

That spring I'd leave the screen door wide
        so regularly
the raccoon could visit our kitchen

because it was hungry, & because we understood,

we left bowls of cereal for it as if it were
        domesticated,
though it never let us pet it, never accepted

our affection. It was a welcome distraction

from the enraged words we'd hung on the walls.
        It wore its fur
stole with aplomb, & like a teenager

rarely raised its face to reveal its mask.

It was always afternoon; the raccoon
        may have been
rabid or dangerous, surely, but I maintain

it was hungry, it was wanting, & that we understood.

The Asymmetry of Time

Down the hill from the schoolyard where seventh graders
squander each recess imagining first kisses—a vision
that frightens & excites them equally, they can even point out

the classmate who co-stars in these fantasies, & how they look
askance, embarrassed, when they're caught almost staring—&
further, beyond the closed mills & the blue-collar bar

where the old timers rerun familiar stories, replaying
heroic roles standing up to foremen or fathers or
foreign fighters in Korea & Vietnam, the train yards remain,

long strands of flat cars like beaded necklaces, laid out.
Diesel engines pull some slowly from one siding to another,
setting them out for cargo containers, for consumerism's heavy loads.

Watchmen with flashlights slice up the yard.
Boxcars laden with night's vaporous ink—a darkness that isn't
dark matter, which itself hasn't been proven to exist

though science suggests 27% of the universe is composed of it.
The math doesn't lie. The white boards of physicists
scrawled with numbers & variables. Their belief

a near theology, so much so I visited once a university
where the physics building had stained glass windows featuring
St. Einstein, St. Newton with his apple, St. Galileo, &

St. Copernicus, a communion of scientists—key players
in middle school lesson plans. We learned the periodic table,
a model of the atom, & learned, too, Oppenheimer's sin—

the possibility of a neutron bomb obliterating our city.
At mass we prayed for peace, & silently for desire's fulfillment,
our wish lists of lost parents & records & Rangers victories.

So many lusts in our little worlds. Never once
did our teachers talk with any sort of excitement about the big bang,
about the formal beauty of the Milky Way, the black hole

at its center. What was inside the church bell that went
unused in the tower if not god, which might well be
another name for dark matter. I stayed awake

too late the day before my science final, trying to memorize
each element's symbol & weight. Other nights my body was
a copper wire charged with a thousand watts of desire.

That wanting became a religion. My belief in sex then
its own kind of dark matter—it was all around &
I'd discover it, not soon enough. Sometimes, abashed,

I'd long to vanish, to decrescendo into my desk, to hop
a freight train out of town, the way a protagonist did
in a novel I read that year, taking on a new identity &

so left his nerdy self behind. It was only a fiction.
There was no escape other than time itself,
which physicists have a theory of as well, one

I never fully understood. These are the key mysteries
of a mysterious cosmos, an enigmatic god, & no one—
not my father or the nuns or the lab coats or the priests

with their catechism & confessionals, not the first girl I kissed
(a kiss that only led to more longing, more unrest), & not
the long decades since have taught me anything. Day or night

in certain towns, trains blow their solitary notes
as they approach a crossing, the sound of that howling
wind-like, heard as an echo in the most distant neighborhoods,

the sound nearly tangible, heavy as a name only thought about.
Is it hope for some fulfillment or only nostalgia?
Does it matter? Come morning the local deacon will unlock

the parish sanctuary & stare into the unlit nothingness among the pews,
while astronomy grad students begin leaving the observatory
to tally data later in the afternoon. Equations prove that creation,

like possibility, is ever expanding, yet contraction remains a possibility.
We exist in the middle of it, unable to dream, the constellations
a spread of toy jacks as on schoolyard asphalt, the moon a ball. Imagine

a child wondering how she's going to pick them all up.

The Coming Autumn

Wednesday morning methadone.
                              Opiate light
through storm-fat clouds. A half dozen pilgrims

queued for the clinic's weekly communion,
its sacristy still locked.
The young mother with rheumy eyes—

I almost recognize her bruises & scabs.

The one repetitive narrative I know has nothing
to do with horoscopes or a desire to be clean:
another visit to the confessional, another covenant smashed.

Rather, it's Rumi:
Where there is ruin there is hope for treasure.

So much hurt in a day, who doesn't want

for resolution, or else
                          a balm to make it bearable.
Some days the only sound is traffic passing, gruff
at fifty miles per hour: a Doppler of muffler growl & siren.

Other days it's the incessant engine of mosquitoes,
their one monotonous dirge.
                             I could turn into

the parking lot, beckon that girl,
her skin pale as this page despite August.

Such is temptation.
Such is the past. Loneliness. The company I keep.

I can't save anyone,
                     & she seems to wear the beatitudes
draped over her shoulders, *meek, poor in spirit...*:

I'd provide a good meal or money, just to hear her say *thank you*,
to watch her bow her head
                          before saying grace,
a prayer I can't even imagine. The dry weed stalks

needle her ankles, scratch at all their calves. Leaf shadows
thin & sharp, dark as a rebuke.

Her grin a blend of flirtation & satisfaction
so readily mistaken for affection or gratitude,

the way a toddler, not mine, once pointed out for me
what he called angels,
                         those vulture silhouettes,
ominous & magnificent against morning's endlessness.

Anole

I've held them squirming in my palm
though being hard to catch is a survivor's

stratagem. Camouflage helps, too,

so these little lizards, splay-legged
shift from leaf green to stem brown

in seconds, the way teen girls

changed faces away from home, their skirts
seeming shorter, their eyes scanning

for parents in hopes not to get caught

even as the boys we were looked on,
with our faux halos, our sweating palms.

Approaching Thanksgiving

The half-moon tonight almost quotidian &
in its ambience, the darker part also visible
so the whole thing resembles a black & white cookie
from those bakeries in Manhattan, & the autumn
air sweet, almost tinged with fennel & the garden's
last mint. Rarely am I taken aback by the celestial
or by the chilly blade November carries
along the night streets, like a tough kid, the sullen one
near the ball courts, the one we learned not to cross,
learned to befriend even. I was never good
at childhood, took it all too seriously, back
when I sat on evening stoops, fed sugared crumbs
to the alley rats. At some point I surrendered
my goals of ever playing point guard for the Knicks
or of flying the space shuttle. Some nights the moon
glowed orange & full as a basketball, & well past
the last pick-up game, tough guy Tyrone'd practice
jump shots from all sides of the asphalt court.
Nobody cared or complained. The thump thump thump—
three dribbles followed by an extended pause before
his feet touched ground again. Sometimes
the rattle of ball against backboard, sometimes
only the nonexistent net's silent swish.
Then the rubber on pavement again, reverberating.
Practice, the sky seemed to say. He rehearsed
arc & angle, practiced a look that said
Don't fuck with me. Even that was a head fake.
He also studied the hustle, like his uncle,
another neighborhood notable, who called me
kid, & who watched my lay-up & declared
I'd never have game. He made that clear
on what was, in retrospect, my first day of adulthood,
the fresh ball circumspect in my small hands.
A blown fast break, another time my team lost.
Because I believed in the democracy of the key,

believed, too, in grace, I took to watching from behind
the chainlink as b-boys dunked & defended,
& to cheering each bounce pass & alley-oop;
how they trusted each other not to call fouls
unless blatant, bloodying. Their movements
all skill & strength, bodies sweat-slick & lit. Maybe
I'd watch until moonrise beckoned streetlights
awake. I knew the bakeries would be closing shop,
the sweets discounted. The cookies I'd buy then,
soft & cakey, just the way they were made
in the old world, an undercurrent of anise
in the batter, the two frostings, each delicious,
each with its own insignificant sweetness.

Solstice

Earlier, the sun turned around, began its long sojourn south.
The neighborhood dogs dream of sirloin & belly rubs.

Or else I'm projecting again, which has been known
to happen, particularly on nights like this

when a few glowing windows reveal shadow-dramatic scenes.
When the asphalt releases its exasperated heat.

When whatever wind the mountain exhales, ruffles loose
the last delicate scents of honeysuckle.

When a Northern Saw-whet circles for rabbit
then circles again, wings open to air streams.

Tonight, only a white stripe of skunk, nearly radiant
among the garden vegetables—

its slick, black fur smudged to inky night.
In a driveway, an RV shakes with adolescent laughter.

Hunger & more hunger—what motivates the beasts of the world.
In another century, another city, one redundant with distant light,

I would wake in my room, wanting—
my mother on the far side of the house typing dictation.

I could hear the muffled staccato of each sentence.
My brother & sister asleep. Staring at me from across the room,

the taxidermied owl someone believed the perfect gift for a child
talons open as if it might pluck from my chest the nightmares,

the longing, the very poetry.
How it might feast, then fly in a maelstrom of viscera &

that I would learn to follow even into this latest of decades
for want of what had been taken.

On Hearing Word of her Death

It made the news—the local papers, at least;
a friend sent me the article, asked
whether it could be the same J—,

her body found half-naked, eyes blackened
with smudged mascara. The story mentioned
no family, no suspects. She'd always lived

dangerously—a junkie ex, a dealer ex,
who'd given her the pager she kept in her purse
even when we'd dated. How his eyes on me,

if he'd see us together, glinted
like switchblade blades revealed to sunlight.
I loved that. Remember

how in a national park renown for being
scenic, she undid my jeans, got to her knees
as a waterfall played its scherzo cello

not far away. We were cited
for being unnatural among the nature trails:
another summons for the collection.

How we tried to emigrate to a nation
that might accept us, refugees both
leaving dysfunction & failures behind

or so we believed. In Montreal she begged
me to bind her to the bed posts, back
when I still wore ties, & she called my name

& to Jesus & to any other of god's nom
de plumes, each petit mort a sign,
we told ourselves of long-term potential.

How I used to caress the scar under her
left breast, a scalpel's signature, with my thumb
as if it were possible to gently erase it. I learned how

to stroke her ear lobe when she sobbed
those nights she woke up shaking.
Other nights she insisted she *treasured* me,

that was her word: something secret, to be buried.
No surprise, she settled into restlessness, into that
need for risk, a tryst with a wild-haired waitress

an escape from the respectable home
we'd tried to create. What had happened
to her, I'd sometimes wonder—her face

not on Facebook. I didn't Google ever
even when I yearned for her again, nights
the loneliness accumulated like dust.

In the accompanying photo, dimples still defined
her smile, her eyes retained the same
downcast reticence I'd seen in her father's

the few times we'd met. I was surprised
by her age for in memory she remained forever
twenty-something, not in her forties.

I wanted her again—her sweat & drive, all
flesh & tongue & license that reduced our names
to syllables—or maybe I wanted only that

liberty to trespass, that restless desire to give in
to desire whenever it arrived, how alive
we'd both felt in those months of first touch.

A Slight Misunderstanding

What I heard was that she was interested
in *accidents*, so I envisioned those frozen moments
(perhaps only milliseconds), the liminal frames
when we realize an event is unavoidable,

& then it happens for there's nothing we can do
to prevent such cataclysm:
the precarious slip from the top step;
the glass sliding out of our fingers because

it's condensation-slick, our hand damp;
the helplessness of the right foot
when we stomp the pedal only to feel
the car continue its slide along black ice.

The accompanying sick-to-the-stomach spasm
awaiting crash, the shattering of windshield,
crunch of metal, futility of honed reflexes.
One time I managed to catch a falling tumbler

only to have it surprise itself into a hundred splinters
in my palm & fingers, the subsequent rush to the ER,
twenty-three tweezer tugs. How wrong I was.
What she had said was *accidence*, & by that

I now know she meant chance or happenstance,
the sheer coincidence of occurrence: that we'd be
in the same bar, though we hadn't seen each other
in nearly ten years, so that at first glance I couldn't say

who she was, I'd just accidently overheard that phrase
& turned. My whiskey glass clutched tight
when she waved shyly, eyes down, that ambivalent-
but-glad gesture some make at such moments.

Centuries ago they might have called this fate,
some reason to change our situations. *I'd been thinking
of you just today*, she mentioned. The band played
covers from the 1980s, heightening a sense of nostalgia

for everyone: The Cure's "Pictures of You" right then—
a song from the year she was born. A song already
about longing & distance. One I never really liked,
but she swayed to its rhythm

while around us others sang along
holding one another. We had to move close to speak.
If you feel so lucky, maybe you should play the lottery,
her sister said, that cliche way we all want fortune

to lead to better fortune, for opportunity
to open up to more opportunity. So television's taught.
Rom-coms, too. Her smile, I will say, remained
enigmatic & seductive both, & I remembered

I once described her as inscrutable. A compliment,
I maintain. When they left, I felt glad
to have seen her again, & to have relived those months of
not flirting because it had never been about desire

despite her sister's teasing. *A happy accident*, she said
before leaving. How right she was, I thought, driving
the rainslick streets home, the car hydroplaning slightly
as if to remind me of all the things we can't control.

Big Brown Bat

Having grown up on Bela Lugosi, I think
the name a misnomer——their wingspans average

only twelve inches. She studies their migrations
I tell her how one night a bat soared from

living room to kitchen, & back again.
Wingwind grazing my ear. It had found a crevice,

climbed inside. I don't mention the tennis racquet
or the way I carried its startled furry body outside,

a furiously pulsing half ounce. In those movies,
there's often a scientist & someone who needs saving.

Ditto a romantic subplot & the risk of failure.
Echo location: if I'd opened a window it'd have flown

right out. So confused it must have been. Frightened.
I recall only its wildly beating (like a heart) wings.

It's Christmas. The turkey vultures
        —For Michael and Barbara

It's Christmas. The turkey vultures
have climbed into the choir loft of a nearby tree,
seven, twelve, fifteen of them ready for carols
we are too far to hear. The look sharp
backlit in their black frocks, their monastic heads
bowed & serious. All their songs in minor keys.
Across the street another five have alighted
like Santa's reindeer on a neighbor's roof.
Some omen. Some harbinger. They remain
unfazed by flashing lights, by inflatable snowmen
suddenly resuscitated, by the old world
curses of a grandfather worried about
evil eyes & wives' tales. These are beaks that know
carrion, talons that carry death over
backyards, patios, children pointing them out.
Winged, ferocious, hideous & full of grace
they could be seraphim. We are
miles from steeple or cemetery.
The community's lone lake remains ice-scabbed.
The gazebo overlooking it frowns despite
its crown of holiday lights, each bulb a blazing
scarab. There are no crows or pigeons,
only the vultures. Already,
the remains of gift giving burn in fireplaces—
hearth smoke & kitchen scents mingling.
My brother wants to know what can be done
about the buzzards, talks about shooting them
with garden hose spray or shaking that tree
viciously, for they are awful & ugly & blessed all
at once, & like any of us, clutching carnage &
redemption both, our redundant lists
of naughty & nice. How radiant
the afternoon sky in the bay window, even
as occasional shadows darken the welcome mat.

O Holy Night

The tiny novitiates of candlelight flicker but remain
devout despite the bedroom's draft,

the movement of flame a kind of flirtation,
the wicks seeming to wink &

beckon. Tonight was supposed to be
romantic in that way certain movies depict—

But it's easy to forget the body can be
sacred in its carnal wants. Touch, too. I've never been good

at fidelity, so often I've been tempted
by my name called in the hushed & desolate dark.

Up Early, I Turn off the Television News

High tide of sun curling & breaking onto the hardwood
so many fragments of light; coffee fragrant from the kitchen

where the cats mewl coolly by their dishes.
Later, they'll return to their dreams of fresh kills—

feather remnants or mole entrails scattered on the couch,
evidence of another violent yet typical day,

I've seen the way they pursue chickadees come spring.
Even my petty cruelties of callousness & ingratitude

go without acknowledgment or absolution.
Half a world away, in the name of some rebellion,

a belt explodes on a bus, & the young boy holding onto
his mother doesn't have a chance

to cry or call out when her hand is blown from her wrist:
before he can process this absence, his body is

buffeted by shrapnel & shattered metal. Maybe
he was lucky to die with her touch,

her enduring maternal presence, as his last thought,
to be going out with her, to be happy...

The street littered with shards of aluminum & windowpane,
each licked by light 'til they became glowing splinters.

Maybe the driver been thinking right then, without dismay,
about the day's ordinariness to that point,

about the traffic & his boyfriend's near-daily complaints
about watering the plants, or else about his last compliment.

The three old women on their way to market who'd watched
it all, the concussion echoing until it became one

with other conflagrations, other carnage in memory,
how calm they seemed on television, discussing it

until I realized they were most likely in shock,
the way they didn't seem to blink or look away from the camera.

If I saw them interviewed, no doubt, so too did the conspirators
who must have congratulated themselves, clapping

without any cruelty in their celebration,
maybe even firing Kalashnikovs in the air, all of them, that is

but one, who perhaps heard about the young boy & recalled
his own son who'd died among the clashes

after another rocket barrage, the shocking detonations.
His desperation a valley with a dry riverbed at its bottom.

He's come to believe in little. Not the U.N. or the benevolence
of American presidents. Not the god of his collaborators.

He no longer believes in poetry, doesn't buy into
the righteousness of the cause, for the cause is death. For him

hope is now either an oasis or a mirage
in the long desert history has become, the same

landscape of his forefathers, & the inheritance he'll leave.
Still, the sun, unmediated & complete, eases above

the dwindling olive groves, the withered fig trees of his wife's family,
above, too, the refugee camps & outdoor markets

where feral cats stalk the stalls for mice & scraps,
where street children forage for sweets or coins,

silvery warm as a distant star, & above the antiquities dig
so much like the one on the Discovery channel last night,

where archaeologists dusted sand away from
the mummified remains of an ancient grave site &

the voice-over explained how the team worked
puzzling together a narrative from the smallest pieces,

how the split bones & broken spears showed
these were victims of some great & ancient sorrow.

The Temporary World

The water tranquil, soft loll of sunglaze
as one sailboat lazes from its dock toward adventure
beyond the bay.
Isn't this how so many stories begin? Behind me

all tumult—jackhammers & Harley growl,
shrieks of children, their laughter gift wrapped
in golden light.
The old oaks chaperone, wear boas of Spanish moss.

Anoles have gone into hiding among
the underbrush: I even watched one leap, an Olympian,
from the sidewalk,
before it changed from brown to green

the way they will, adaptation necessary
for survival, to avoid workmen sawing away dead fronds
& the wrens that
woke me earlier, which seem harmless enough

seeing as they're barely fist-sized,
their beaks almost dainty. But deadly. Such deception
shouldn't shock us.
When it closed its eyes that lizard disappeared.

The school kids have returned to classrooms,
but before they left the cutest one said, *Fuck no!*,
so natural
a reaction when summoned back. In only minutes

the bay's begun to churn, foam gathering
along the water's edge, & the child-drawn clouds
to the south furrow
their brows, portent to a storm I still can't fathom,

so that, hours from now, rain will lash
the windows, breakers crash beyond the storm wall.
Imagine those lizards:
how important to survival it is for them to hold on,

the way they cling to some quavering branch.

The Ever After

For a chapel the hotel's set up
a small meeting room
overlooking the riverwalk,
with ribboned chairs, bunting,
cut calla lilies in vases pale
among the Tampa suntans,
so that out past the pastor
you'll see during the ceremony
a few punts & some tourist
boats on the currents.
The first guests have already
arrived, mingle among grooms-
men in funereal black,
bridesmaids in dresses the color
of currants, corsages, red sashes.
From the lobby bar I've bought
a whiskey to this table so I might
watch, everyone hopeful, though
we all know of horror stories—
the newlywed wife who admits
on her honeymoon of another man
whom she adores, the husband
who begins drinking the night of
I now pronounce you...
& just doesn't stop. Google
shortest marriages if you must.
Up comes a caché of calamities.
Still, the invited arrive in their finery.
Still, the minister blesses them &
their lives together. Whatever
the adverb, there's an ever after.
My friends at the bar—how they
choose to meet each other
whenever & wherever they can
despite the 600 miles

that separate them, despite
past divorces, the bad breaks
& more bad break ups. Stella kept
her wedding portrait on the wall
for nearly fifty years after
my Uncle John passed. She never
dated again. How she missed
his laugh. How she missed dancing.
You should have seen her:
every family wedding, she polka-ed
in the arms of cousins, nephews,
in-laws. It's what we hope for,
such devotion: those single women
ready to wrestle for a bouquet,
those guests with their gifts,
their good wishes. Thus I watch
despite my scabs & the hurts
I've bestowed on others—
my willful flaws, my feeble spirit—
but duck out before the kiss, leave
them to remain betrothed for
longer in my mind, *in love.*
Later, I see the groom, bow tie
loose from celebration & shake
his hand for happiness—
his & his wife's or my own?
Doesn't matter. Reception music
echoes in the corridor &
I consider whether to crash it,
to dance a single song with one
of the sad lonely women
there for no other reason than
the joy such movement brings,
the spark of momentary touch,
rhythm & sweat & so much cheering.
Clink of spoon on glass. My friends
have already gone to their room

& you are nothing but a ghost,
old loneliness, imagined friend
I've pal-ed around with for decades.
I raise my glass *'til death do us part.*
Workers have left the chairs up
in that makeshift chapel; in silhouette,
their stiff curved backs like
rows of headstones, & behind them
the dark window, the darker river,
small lights on its other side.

Club Soda

Back then few of us could afford a beach
thus, we rarely came out before dusk,
that summer of poems & guitar feedback,

of bouncer shifts & women who stopped by
the club after stripper stints on a ramshackle stage
east of town, a place called Glamorz—

with a Z—where I'd never been. Consecutively,
I had a crush on each of them although
now I only recall Stacey who had an acne rash

along her left cheek & whose hair was a paragraph
about raven feathers. Her voice all cigarettes &
bad men: absent father, abusive brothers, cruel

bosses, the list goes on. In the bar some nights
I had to play boyfriend in order to prevent a drunk
from getting handsy & angry, sweat on his forehead

as on a beer bottle. The air conditioners futile.
This was Kalamazoo & decades ago, & what became
of Paul the barman, my fellow bouncers, the regulars,

or Stacey—I can't say. I kissed her one time
all mouth & tongue because I had to, kissed her until
on the stool beside her the guy grunted, barged out,

& still we kissed. Then Paul cleared his throat.
That was nice, she said. Nice was something
she didn't know, something I wasn't sure I wanted to be,

but I felt, for a moment, a kind of wealth
I'd never known. Her skin, gritty, the color of sand,
I could smell the salt that had dried on her neck.

Her smile a cat that followed me beyond last call
after which I walked into the bar cooler,
hauled empty kegs as my shaking hands numbed.

There was no relief outside that cold solitude:
outside remained July, the night humid without
forecast rain even though my pulse was all thunder,

even though a raptor inside me struggled to fly off.

Dog

We weren't pure breeds. We were
Iggy Pop dogs—mutts, mongrels, the ones

that jumped fences, busted out of pounds. Sure
we snarled & growled, desperate

as vagrants. We knocked over trash cans
& gnawed through garbage bags.

Pet us once & we rarely snapped again–
such was our adolescence: throw us a biscuit

we'd follow you home, ready— not for the collar—
but for a pat on the head, to hear you say, *good boy*.

Pet Sounds

Rag top weather. End-of-summer
balanced on the splayed knuckles
of Appalachia. No one here hoards
surf wax or hauls a boogie board
on roof racks of old Fords.
This ain't California. Because
in the market all the talk's of ragweed
or the looming school year or love
—it's finality; its fragility—today
I won't pull over for roadside ice cream.
Let the engine whine: flywheel &
overdrive; rocker arms rocking.
Let wind sweep & acceleration
be my rock 'n' roll. Because I know,
too, the failure of words, believe in it,
actually, I want an instrumental.
The roadster crests another hill;
I steer into an S curve as if barreling
a wave, the maple leaves almost foamy
in the white heat. Even Brian Wilson
understood some moments refuse
harmony, refuse melody, refuse a refrain.
My hair brushed back as if by a woman,
the brow sweat drying, salt
sticky like beach day aftermath.
The road dips & ascends again—
the engine revving, revving
like late night juke box picks,
like your heart rate the first time
you fall in love with a song.

Here, Today

A brand-new love affair is such a beautiful thing...

With hair the color & texture of grackle feathers
the woman at the table beside mine waves
to a friend on the street. I've fallen in love
with Dublin today, even with the cackle & *caw*
caw of seagulls on St. Stephen's Green,
which could be the name of a shade of green
noticeably different than St. Anne's Green or
Phoenix Park green. I've fallen in love, too,
with the way raindrops freckle the sidewalks
one moment, then sunlight sets the whiskey
in my tumbler luminous. As well with the word
tumbler, which I will not investigate the origins of.
I want to raise my glass to that woman,
not because I find her attractive or I'm lonely
in the way of tourists & transients, but because
we're both here, today, a Thursday, afternoon
& our waiter has left us alone. Lovers
parade past, walking close, even that pair of seniors—
how gently he holds her arm to steady her.
Maybe Tony Asher got it wrong. I could watch
musicians play songs their fathers knew,
their grandfathers, or else see the Blackrock
Boys cover the Ventures, Jan & Dean, the Surfaris,
the Beach Boys. They insist the surfing's great
a bus ride away in Dublin Bay, no need
to go to the west coast despite the famous swells
off Donegal & Sligo. Everything old is new again
or so the saying goes, even this city,
even desire, even the green that fills
the sycamores so that I want nothing more
than to be here, by myself, where the faint
keyboard & guitar & tambourine tumble from
a neighboring pub when the door opens,
the Blackrock Boys imploring in harmony

with slight accents we *keep in mind love is here, today*
tomorrow it's gone. Or I'll be gone. There's only
this moment. I can't bear to try a whiskey
called Writer's Tears, but I've tasted the Red Breast,
the Yellow Spot, the Method and Madness. How
satisfying this Green Spot's sweet smolder when
I take another sip. I've fallen in love with anonymity.
At the other table only her empty wine glass
remains, pink lipstick on its rim the only kiss.

Security

The man in the Explosive Specialist shirt
mentions he's Secret Service not TSA

summoned from some hidden terminal
room to search my bags, talk me through

the process. My carry-on flagged for protein
bars that might be plastique, & I failed

the swab test, some residue battery acid
or fertilizer on my fingertips. I'm lucky

my passport's blue though it's summer so
I'm swarthier than usual. Like crows

hovering fresh carrion, so many gawkers
—heading for vacation, heading for home—

have gathered. They point. They whisper.
Who knew excitement might start before

boarding? Will they look for me on their planes?
It doesn't help I've packed several copies of

The Story of Ash among shirts & socks.
It's not a manifesto, I assure. Four other agents

ransack the backpack my laptop's in,
not one cracks a joke. I'm lucky

I'm white. I know. They're looking out
for me, I tell myself. I do believe that

despite news stories of ICE & border agents
every uniform isn't bad. In their badge photos

they're smiling, each of them. One explains
how he'll pat me down with the back of his hands,

now; later in another room after another failure
it'll be palms that search my arms & legs,

ankles & waistband. They won't be frowning,
just serious, wary. I worry too much. They find

nada for there's nothing to find. It's due diligence.
I put my shoes back on. My belt. Re-pack my luggage.

I'm leaving the United States for a few weeks,
but I'll be back, I whisper, almost a warning.

Sex and Death Since the Age Fourteen

I knew I couldn't step outside without notice
so instead I went to the basement with its stale reek
of heating oil & mildew, & rooted through
boxes of the dead man's things, & there
found the first photos I'd ever seen of men & women
naked outside picture of Eden in the family Bible—
Eve's heavy maternal breasts, the tiny serpent's head
that was Adam's penis. These, though, were glossy,
vivid, sexy in a way I understood to be a sin, & knew
I wanted. Even if I knew it were wrong, I took two
& folded them till they were small enough to hide away.
Thus began my study of a biology ignored
at St. Charles School, though I imagined my classmates,
each no less pretty than the next, & imagined, too,
the young widow who'd asked me to keep an eye on her
two sons a few nights. Her name was Bonnie,
& she was just that, *bonny*, meaning pleasing to the eye.
I hadn't thought of her in decades, though I admit
I dreamt of her then & woke sweating, desirous,
not because I'd seen her in a bikini that one time
but because she was kind to me & touched my hand
for a second too long when she paid my wage.
Out the window of my room at 3 in the morning
little moved, & a streetlight did its silent persistent work.
Somewhere, I was certain, men & women touched each other
in the ways of those photographs, just not in our apartment
nor in Bonnie's. This was 1982, the year of teen sex
movies—*Porky's & The Last American Virgin*—& everyone
at the bus stops & birthday parties & pizzerias talked
about how they almost did it, or who did it & who
didn't. We lived in a world of lies & of wanting,
of the stories told until they became real enough,
a world of longing & more longing, which can become
a kind of faith, & we its missionaries. Tell me today's different
& I'll call you a liar. The body continues to wake me

in the darkest hours, & I continue to recite to no one
the rosary of sins, revel in the decades the details I barely
recall, how I must make them up even
before recounting, too, like sheep, my virtues.
The streets empty as the unlit eyes of the stained glass
martyrs & saints of the local church: impossible
role models, we never became those either. How unsurprising
to see my neighbor across the street, curtains open,
watching porn on her television, accepting the body's
own sacred lonesomeness, its troublesome, unrelenting
yearning. I know enough to turn away, to allow
the private hungers to remain confined to those
confidential chambers. Wind fingers the porch chimes
which sing like consecration bells, a piercing amen.

AWARD-WINNING WRITER GERRY LAFEMINA is the author of over twenty books, most recently *The Pursuit: A Meditation on Happiness* (creative nonfiction) and *Baby Steps for Doomsday Prepping* (prose poems). His previous books include a novel, a collection of short stories, and numerous collections of poetry, including *The Parakeets of Brooklyn, Vanishing Horizon, Little Heretic,* and *The Story of Ash.* His essays on poets and prosody, *Palpable Magic,* came out on Stephen F. Austin University Press and his textbook, *Composing Poetry: A Guide to Writing Poems and Thinking Lyrically* was released by Kendall Hunt. Among his awards and honors is a Pushcart Prize, a Michigan Council for the Arts and Cultural Affairs Fellowship, and an Irving Gilmore Foundation grant. A noted literary arts activist who has served on the Board of Directors of the AWP and edited numerous literary journals and anthologies, LaFemina is the former director of the Center for Literary Arts at Frostburg State University, where he is a Professor of English, serves as a Mentor in the MFA Program at Carlow University and is a current Fulbright Specialist in Writing, Literature, and American Culture. In his "off" time he is the principle song writer and front man for Coffin Curse recording artists, The Downstrokes.